Editor
Stephanie Buehler, Psy.D.

Contributing Editor
Wanda Kelly

Managing Editor
Ina Massler Levin, M.A.

Editor-in-Chief
Sharon Coan, M.S. Ed.

Cover Artist
Barb Lorseyedi

Art Director
CJae Froshay

Art Coordinator
Kevin Barnes

Imaging
Ralph Olmedo, Jr.

Product Manager
Phil Garcia

Publishers
Rachelle Cracchiolo, M.S. Ed.
Mary Dupuy Smith, M.S. Ed.

Writing Paragraphs

GRADE 2

Author

Wanda Kelly

Teacher Created Materials, Inc.
6421 Industry Way
Westminster, CA 92683
www.teachercreated.com.

ISBN-0-7439-3341-9

©2002 Teacher Created Materials, Inc.
Reprinted, 2004
Made in U.S.A.

Table of Contents

Introduction

The old adage "practice makes perfect" can really hold true for your child and his or her education. The more practice and exposure your child has with concepts being taught in school, the more success he or she is likely to find. For many parents, knowing how to help their children may be frustrating because the resources may not be readily available.

Practice Makes Perfect: Writing Paragraphs, Grade 2, is a resource to help students practice and reinforce skills taught in the classroom. This book presents paragraph skills that is appropriate for second graders.

The book is divided into seven main sections. Each of those sections is based on one of the following objectives that second grade students should meet:

- Plan a paragraph (discuss ideas, list ideas) before beginning to write.
- Use a logical organization.
- Revise a paragraph by varying sentence structure and by adding specific details and eliminating irrelevant ones.
- Proof a paragraph to check for correct grammar, punctuation, capitalization, and spelling.
- Edit a paragraph to improve organization, sentence structure, and word choice.

A review section at the beginning of the book covers some of the basics of writing: kinds of sentences; the correct use of punctuation, grammar, and capitalization; and spelling. Following the review, there are exercises that provide practice in paragraph planning and organizing, revising, proofing, and editing. Attention is also given to individual sentence structure and content within paragraphs as well as the mechanics of writing: grammar, punctuation, capitalization, and spelling.

At the end of each section, there are assessments to evaluate a student's progress in each of the skills practiced (planning, organizing, revising, proofing, and editing). At the end of the book, a final assessment covers all five skills. It is in a standardized test format to help students practice test-taking as well as paragraph writing skills. In addition, there is an assessment that requires the student to write an original paragraph. Finally, there is an answer key for each of the practice exercises in the book.

How to Make the Most of This Book

Here are some useful ideas for making the most of this book:

- Set aside a specific place in your home to work on this book. Keep it neat and tidy, with the necessary materials on hand.
- Set up a certain time of day to work on these practice pages to establish consistency; or look for times in your day or week that are less hectic and conducive to practicing skills.
- Keep all practice sessions with your child positive and constructive. If your child becomes frustrated or tense, set the book aside and look for another time to practice. Forcing your child to perform will not help. Do not use this book as a punishment.
- Help beginning readers with instructions.
- Review the work your child has done.
- Pay attention to the areas in which your child has the most difficulty. Provide extra guidance and exercises in those areas.
- Look for ways to make real-life application to the skills being reinforced.

A Quick Review

Sentences and Punctuation

- Every sentence must have at least one subject and at least one verb or predicate.
  ex.: Jamie *(subject)* runs *(verb/predicate).*

- Every sentence must begin with a capital letter and have a punctuation mark at the end.
  A *declarative* sentence makes a statement and ends with a period.

  ex.: Jamie runs very fast.

  An *interrogative* sentence asks a question and ends with a question mark.

  ex.: Does Jamie run very fast?

  An *imperative* sentence makes a command and ends with a period.

  ex.: Do not run, Jamie.

  An *exclamatory* sentence shows strong emotion and ends with an exclamation point.

  ex.: Run, Jamie!

Capitalization

- Begin particular names, specific places, and the names of days of the week, months, and holidays with capital letters.
  Names: Desmond, Carlos, Cecilia, Benny

  Places: Richmond, Virginia, Europe, Lake Erie, Pacific Ocean, Rainbow County

  Days, Months, and Holidays: Saturday, February, Independence Day

Grammar

- *Verbs* and *subjects* must agree.
  ex.: Ricardo runs. He runs. Ricardo and Rosa run. They run.

- Use *verbs* in sentences to tell how a subject acts or feels.
  ex.: Rosa walked home. Rosa felt sad.

- Add *descriptive words* to sentences to make them more interesting and to give more information.
  ex.: Rosa **quickly** walked. Rosa felt **sad**.

Spelling

- Check in a dictionary if you are not sure of the exact spelling of a word. Learn some of the basic spelling rules.
  ex.: One rule is that **i** comes before **e** except after **c**. *(niece, ceiling)*

Assessing the Basics

Sentences, Punctuation, and Capitalization

Write the following sentences with the correct capitalization and punctuation. Then circle the kind of sentence each is: declarative, interrogative, imperative, exclamatory.

1. i saw danny in dayton, ohio

_____

| declarative | imperative | interrogative | exclamatory |

2. did you see fran in dallas, texas

_____

| imperative | declarative | interrogative | exclamatory |

3. do not go to europe by yourself

_____

| interrogative | imperative | exclamatory | declarative |

4. what a great time they had

_____

| exclamatory | declarative | interrogative | imperative |

Grammar and Spelling

Choose the correct forms of the verbs. Also correct any spelling errors when you rewrite the following sentences.

5. Jan and Vicky (run/runs) in razes.

_____

6. She (run/runs) fastier than he dos.

_____

7. Gwen and George carefuly (steps/stepped) into the gleaming red cirkus wagen.

_____

Put Details in Order

The lists below contain details that you can use to write two different paragraphs. Put each group of details in order by numbering them one through seven.

Mornings

_____ wake up

_____ eat breakfast

_____ catch bus

_____ get dressed

_____ comb hair

_____ wash face

_____ hang up towel

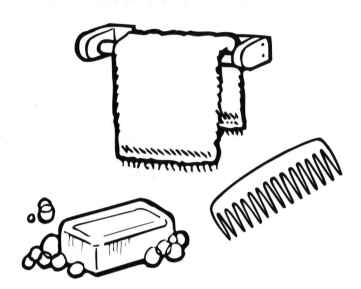

Baking a Cake

_____ mix batter

_____ measure ingredients

_____ find recipe

_____ preheat oven

_____ put cake in oven

_____ gather ingredients

_____ pour batter in pan

Choose a Topic and List Ideas

The first step in writing a paragraph is choosing a topic, or a subject you would like to write about. Then, you make a list of ideas or details to use in writing about that topic.

In the Topics Bank is a list of four topics about which you might choose to write. Below the bank are four lists of ideas or details. First, write the correct topic above each list. Then, add one idea to each list.

Topics Bank

Favorite Rides	**School**
Ice Cream	**Summer**

---

1. _____

creamy, cold, and sweet
banana splits
strawberry sundaes

_____

3. _____

swimming
ice-cold drinks
vacations

_____

2. _____

roller coasters
loop rides
spinning rides

_____

4. _____

recess
subjects
teacher

_____

Choose a Topic and List Ideas (cont.)

List three ideas or details you could use to write a paragraph for each of the following topics.

Assessment: 1

In the box below, there are three topics and nine supporting details (three for each topic). Put the topic on the first line and then list the supporting details below it.

Topics and Supporting Details

nature programs

keeps me company

Best Subjects

easy to please

Disney movies

math

Television Shows

goes everywhere with me

Saturday morning cartoons

language arts

My Pet

social studies

---

1. _____

   _____

   _____

   _____

2. _____

   _____

   _____

   _____

3. _____

   _____

   _____

   _____

Assessment: 2

In the box below, there are three topics and nine supporting details (three for each topic). Put the topic on the first line and then list the supporting details below it.

Topics and Supporting Details

marathon	two years older
gymnastics	Our House
Olympics Events	friendly neighborhood
on a quiet street	teases me
helps me with math	swimming
My Brother	large family room

---

1. _____

   _____

   _____

   _____

2. _____

   _____

   _____

   _____

3. _____

   _____

   _____

   _____

Assessment: 3

There are three topics and nine supporting details (three for each topic). Put the topics on the lines after the numbers and list the supporting details under the appropriate topics.

Topics and Supporting Details

snowball fights	**bake cookies**
write letters	**ride sleds**
spend some, save some	**paid weekly**
make snowmen	**Rainy-day Activities**
read books	**My Allowance**
have to earn it	**Winter Activities**

1. _____

   _____

   _____

   _____

2. _____

   _____

   _____

   _____

3. _____

   _____

   _____

   _____

Topic Sentences

A paragraph begins with a *topic sentence* that tells the reader what the paragraph will be about. Provide topic sentences for these paragraphs.

1. _____

   _____

Looking fluffy and white like pillows, they are gooey and sweet when I bite into them. After roasted over a fire, they are crunchy on the outside and sweet on the inside. If I could, I would eat a hundred marshmallows for breakfast.

2. _____

   _____

My cat can fall asleep anywhere and anytime. One time she fell asleep inside my dad's boot. Another time she fell asleep while I was brushing her fur. Yesterday, she crawled into my sock drawer and slept there all day. Today I changed her name from Frisky to Sleepy.

3. _____

   _____

First, I do not like getting into the water because it is cold. Just trying to move in the water makes me tired very fast. I also hate it when I sink to the bottom of the pool. My final dislike is the awful odor and taste of chlorine. I think I am going to take karate lessons instead of swimming lessons.

Supporting Sentences

Supporting details add more information about the topic. They come in the middle of a paragraph. Add one supporting sentence to each paragraph.

1. How to Make Parents Unhappy

If you want to make your parents unhappy, keep your room as messy as possible. Do not put away your clothes. Instead, throw them on the furniture and the floor. Eat pizza in your room, and leave the carton on the floor.

_____

_____

These are some good ways to make sure that your parents are upset with you.

2. Dogs: Better Pets Than Cats

I like dogs better than cats. My dog will always come to me when I call him, but my cat just comes to me whenever she feels like it. When I am sad, my dog seems to understand and feel sorry for me. My cat is always the same when I am happy or sad. I can teach my dog how to jump and catch a Frisbee, but my cat is not interested in doing anything I want to teach her.

_____

_____

If I had to choose, I would rather have a dog than a cat.

Concluding Sentences

A *concluding sentence* restates the main idea of the paragraph. It comes at the end of a paragraph. Add a concluding sentence at the end of each paragraph.

1. School: Its Good Points

School does have its good points. Everyone knows that it is a good idea to learn as much as possible. There are other good things about school, too. It is a place where I can meet many different people and make good friends. At my school, I also can play games and exercise.

_____

_____

2. Firefighters: Strong and Brave

Firefighters are both strong and brave. They have to be strong to wear their heavy equipment and to work with the ladders and hoses. Every firefighter has to be prepared to go inside a burning building to rescue people and to put out fires. That means being brave.

_____

_____

Ordering Paragraph Sentences

Read the sentences for a paragraph titled "My Allowance" below and label them as follows:

T The **topic sentence** states the main idea to the paragraph

S The **supporting sentences** gives specific details about the topic

C The **concluding sentence** restates the main idea the paragraph

Once you have labeled the sentences, write them in the correct order on the lines below to form the paragraph.

My Allowance

_____ 1. One of the things I usually need is school supplies.

_____ 2. The first thing I do is to put half my allowance in my savings account.

_____ 3. Every week my parents pay me an allowance for doing chores.

_____ 4. I use the remaining half to buy things I need.

_____ 5. Another thing on which I spend my allowance is a book I want to read and keep.

_____ 6. Earning an allowance gives me money to spend and money to save.

_____

_____

_____

_____

_____

_____

Ordering Paragraph Sentences (cont.)

Read the sentences for the paragraph below. Write your own topic sentence and label the other sentences as follows:

S The **supporting sentences** gives information about the topic.

C The **concluding sentence** summarizes the paragraph.

Then write the sentences in the correct order to form the paragraph.

Rainy-Day Pleasures

Topic Sentence

_____

_____

_____ 1. After I have made my favorite chocolate cookies, I find a good book to read.

_____ 2. My favorite books are adventure stories.

_____ 3. The very first thing I do is write a letter to my Grandmother Lucille.

_____ 4. My next activity of the day is to make two dozen delicious cookies.

_____ 5. She lives far away in London, England.

_____ 6. These pleasures keep me busy for an entire rainy day.

_____

_____

_____

_____

_____

_____

_____

Ordering Paragraph Sentences (cont.)

Put the *supporting sentences* in the correct order, numbering 1 to 4.

Write an appropriate *topic sentence* for the supporting details.

Write an appropriate *concluding sentence* for the paragraph.

Playing in the Snow

Topic Sentence

_____

_____

_____ First, Leslie and I have snowball fights.

_____ Then, after we build a snowman, we ride down the hill on our sleds.

_____ Next, we do one of our favorite projects.

_____ We build a snowman.

Conclusion _____

_____

Assessment

Number each set of sentences in the correct order. Number the beginning sentence as **1**, the three supporting sentences in order (**2, 3, 4**), and the concluding sentence as **5**.

Rainy Days

_____ The first thing I like to do on rainy days is bake cookies.

_____ Next, I like to write letters to my grandmothers.

_____ I like to do three things on rainy days.

_____ After I have finished baking and writing, I like to read.

_____ When I do these three things, I like rainy days.

Homework Afternoons

_____ After I have done all of those things, I put my books away for the day.

_____ Each day I have three kinds of homework I have to do.

_____ Next, I have to work 20 problems for mathematics.

_____ First, I have to study 20 spelling words.

_____ My last task is to write 20 sentences for language arts.

Our Excellent House

_____ Our house has some rooms I like better than others.

_____ My second favorite room is the kitchen.

_____ My favorite room of all is the family room.

_____ Last, I think my bedroom is one of the best places to be.

_____ With rooms like these, I feel lucky to live in our house.

A Quick Review

Connecting words *(conjunctions)* are words that you can use to make two sentences into one. Look at the examples in the box.

and	I pick oranges.	I pick apples.	I pick oranges and apples.
or	I like bananas.	I like pears.	I like bananas or pears.
but	I eat grapes.	I do not eat figs.	I eat grapes but not figs.

Make the following pairs of sentences into one sentence with the connecting words.

1. **but**   Everyone went to the movie.
             Shawn did not.

_____

2. **or**   Do you want to roller skate?
          Do you want to play soccer?

_____

3. **and**   I know how to read.
            I know how to write.

_____

4. **or**   Would you like milk?
          Would you like water?

_____

Writing Sentences in Different Ways

Paragraphs are more interesting when sentences do not all begin with the same words. Change the sentences in "My Early Morning" so that each one starts in a different way. You may use conjunctions (connecting words) such as *and*, *but*, and *or* to make two sentences into one sentence.

Examples:	I practice the piano every day. I practice for 30 minutes.
	Every day I practice the piano for 30 minutes.
	or
	For 30 minutes every day, I practice the piano.

My Early Morning

I wake up at six o'clock. I hop out of bed. I get ready for school. I go downstairs. I eat breakfast. I grab my schoolbooks. I go outside to wait for the bus. I sit with my friend Charlotte on the bus. I arrive at school. I walk with my friends Charlotte and Molly to the classroom. I am at the end of my early morning.

_____

_____

_____

_____

_____

_____

_____

_____

Add Details

Some sentences add new information or details about a topic. Choose the sentence that has the correct detail to follow each of the numbered sentences. You should have a complete paragraph when you are finished.

Rainy-Day Activities

Beginning/Topic Sentence: On rainy days, there are three activities that I like to do.

Supporting Sentence 1: The first thing I like to do is write letters.

_____

  a. This is because I have fed my dog.

  b. After all, my mother is busy.

  c. If I get them done first, they will go out in the morning mail.

Supporting Sentence 2: My next rainy-day project is baking cookies.

_____

  a. Our oven heats up really fast.

  b. I sing while I am waiting.

  c. Usually, I make chocolate chip, my favorite.

Supporting Sentence 3: My final project for the day is to read a book.

_____

  a. Sometimes I read again one of my favorites, *The Secret Garden*.

  b. Reading is something we all need to do well.

  c. He said he could not read the sign.

Ending/Closing Sentence: These three activities can keep me busy for an entire rainy day.

Remove Details

One way to *revise* (improve) a paragraph is to take out details that do not add any information about a topic. The sentences in the paragraph below are numbered. Write on the lines following the paragraphs the numbers of the three sentences that do not belong in the paragraph.

Wintertime Fun

Where I live, the winter snows make it easy to do some of my favorite winter activities. **(1)** As soon as I can, I like to go outside to build a snowman. **(2)** Each time, I try to make my snowman bigger than any I have made before. **(3)** Springtime means there will be many flowers in bloom. **(4)** Another thing I like to do in winter is get together with my friends to have snowball fights. **(5)** One time Luke and I had a fight with toy swords. **(6)** We make our snowballs when the snow is not icy so that no one gets hurt. **(7)** Also, in the winter I get to use my sled to slide down hills in the snow. **(8)** Going on summer vacations is fun. **(9)** As soon as fall begins, I start to think about the three things I like to do most when I am outside in the winter.

a. _____   b. _____   c. _____

Assessment

Recall that writing sentences in different ways makes a paragraph more interesting to read. Change the sentences in this paragraph so that none of them begins with the same word. You may combine two sentences into one sentence or change the order of the words in the sentences.

Huckleberry Finn Park

The park I like to go to is Huckleberry Finn Park. The park has 11 different swings. The park has three different slides. The park has other playground equipment. The park has many trees that are easy and fun to climb. The park has a place where I can have a picnic. Huckleberry Finn Park is my favorite park to go to when I want to play and have a picnic.

_____

_____

_____

_____

_____

_____

_____

_____

_____

_____

Assessment (cont.)

When you rewrite the paragraph, leave out the details that do not support the topic sentence.

Camping Is Fun

Camping is fun for many reasons. It is fun to sleep outside or in a tent. The most popular sport in my school is soccer. Food tastes better when it has been cooked over an open fire. One of my favorite camping foods is the s'mores we make with graham crackers, marshmallows, and pieces of chocolate. I can play outside after I clean up my room. Also, it is exciting when I see a deer or another wild animal from my campsite. Besides watching the animals, I like to hike in the woods and fish in the river. If I finish my homework, I can watch my favorite TV show. My dog knows how to shake and sit. At the end of the camping day, I like to sleep in a cozy sleeping bag. All these things make camping fun.

_____

_____

_____

_____

_____

_____

_____

_____

_____

_____

_____

A Quick Review

Rewrite the sentences to make all the corrections necessary.

Example: Marisa and Rollando rides, their bikes to school.

Marisa and Rollando ride their bikes to school.

1. Grant and Stuart puts their toys away every nieght.

_____

2. Nancy run across the streat in front of the Car.

_____

3. Casey do not licke to play with Dolls.

_____

4. yesterday Michael was too sicke to goe to new york.

_____

5. Tooday Ezra also did not feal weel.

_____

6. Will Jenny be ill toomorrow.

_____

7. lets hope thet both of them is okay.

_____

Practice Proofreading a Paragraph

Place a checkmark above the errors you find in the paragraph. Then rewrite it with the corrections you make.

meadow monkeys

in the meadow you will find many aminals, including the harvest mouse. this tiny animal can climd from plant to plant and look just like a Monkey? Harvest mice climd these Plants looking fore food. they eat as much as they can in the suumer to get ready for Winter.

_____

_____

_____

_____

_____

_____

_____

_____

Assessment

Place a checkmark where you find errors in the paragraph. Then rewrite it with the corrections you make.

Snake in the grass

A snake is one of the scariest aminals The grass snake likes to rest in the sun. grass snake eat frogs and newts they live in marshy meadows sometimes the grass snake will pretend to be dead The more you learn about snakes, the lessest scary they are.

_____

_____

_____

_____

_____

_____

_____

_____

Improve Organization

Rewrite the sentences below in the correct order to make a paragraph.

I Need My Sleep

First, I went to my mom's room, but she was still sleeping. Suddenly, I remembered it was Saturday, so I went back to bed! Today I woke up early, got out of bed, and brushed my teeth. I ate breakfast, but then I noticed that it was very quiet. Next, I went to my brother's room, but he was still sleeping too. After that, I put my homework in my backpack. When I went to the porch, I saw that even the dog was still sleeping.

_____

_____

_____

_____

_____

_____

_____

_____

_____

_____

_____

_____

Improve Sentence Structure

Rewrite the following paragraph. Change the order of the words in the sentences and combine sentences so that no sentences begin with the same words.

Kyle and Kate at the Zoo

Kyle and Kate went to the zoo. Kyle and Kate saw many different animals at the zoo. Kyle and Kate first saw a cage filled with rattlesnakes. Kyle and Kate next saw a pen with a mother giraffe and a baby giraffe in it. Kyle and Kate saw a young elephant in the last pen. Kyle and Kate saw the elephant eating peanuts. Kyle and Kate enjoyed seeing all the animals at the city zoo.

_____

_____

_____

_____

_____

_____

_____

_____

_____

_____

_____

_____

Improve Word Choice

You can make a livelier paragraph by using words that describe things or that are more specific.

Example:

Dull: I reached for an apple.

Lively: My eager hand snaked into the big, blue bowl to grab a golden apple.

Complete the paragraph below by adding descriptive or specific words. Use your replacement words when you rewrite the paragraph on a separate sheet of paper.

The _____ Spider

I spied the _____ spider on my

_____ desk. Slowly and _____ , I

sneaked around my _____ desk, looking at the

_____ spider. "What is the spider doing on my

_____ desk?" I thought to myself. Where had the

_____ spider come from? Which one of my

_____ enemies planted the spider on my desk?

As I tiptoed toward my _____ desk, the ugly

spider began to move. I screamed

_____ and dashed from my

_____ room.

Assessment

Rewrite the following paragraph to improve organization, sentence structure, and word choice.

Organization: Put the sentences in the correct order—a topic sentence, supporting sentences, and a concluding sentence.

Sentence Structure: Vary the order of the words in the sentences so that the sentences all have different beginnings.

Word Choice: Add descriptive and specific words to make the topic more interesting.

My Baby Brother

He made another mess by pulling out all the things I had hidden under the bed. He always makes a mess when he gets into my room. My baby brother is a pest. I want him locked out of my room forever. He got into my room yesterday while I was at school. He first took all of the pages out of one of my books. He also got into my closet and pulled all my clothes off the hangers. He should never be allowed to go into my room.

_____

_____

_____

_____

_____

_____

_____

_____

_____

_____

Paragraph Plan: Tell a Story

Make a plan for writing a story paragraph by telling about an experience that you have had—something you did or something that happened. Plan your paragraph by writing a topic sentence, making a list of supporting details, and writing a concluding sentence.

Topic Sentence _____

_____

_____

_____

List of Details _____

_____

_____

_____

_____

_____

_____

_____

Concluding Sentence _____

_____

_____

_____

Tell a Story

Write the title of your story paragraph on the line below. Then use your story paragraph plan as a guide to write your paragraph.

_____

_____

_____

_____

_____

_____

_____

_____

_____

_____

_____

_____

_____

_____

_____

Paragraph Plan:
Explain "How to . . ."

Make a plan for writing a paragraph that explains how to do something, to give facts, or to give directions. Plan your paragraph by writing a topic sentence, making a list of supporting details, and writing a concluding sentence.

Topic Sentence _____

_____

_____

_____

List of Details _____

_____

_____

_____

_____

_____

_____

_____

Concluding Sentence _____

_____

_____

_____

Explain "How to . . ."

Write the title of your paragraph on the line below. Then use your "How to . . ." paragraph plan from page 34 to write your paragraph.

_____

_____

_____

_____

_____

_____

_____

_____

_____

_____

_____

_____

_____

_____

_____

Paragraph Plan: Describe a Person, Place, or Thing

Make a plan for writing a paragraph to describe a person, place, or thing. Plan your paragraph by writing a topic sentence, making a list of supporting details, and writing a concluding sentence.

Topic Sentence _____

_____

_____

_____

List of Details _____

_____

_____

_____

_____

_____

_____

_____

Concluding Sentence _____

_____

_____

_____

Describe a Person, Place, or Thing

Write the title of your paragraph on the line below. Then use your description paragraph plan on page 36 to write your paragraph.

_____

_____

_____

_____

_____

_____

_____

_____

_____

_____

_____

_____

_____

Paragraph Plan: Alike and Different

Make a plan for writing a paragraph to tell how two different objects or people are alike or different in three or four ways. Plan your paragraph by writing a topic sentence, making a list of supporting details, and writing a concluding sentence.

Topic Sentence _____

_____

_____

_____

List of Details _____

_____

_____

_____

_____

_____

_____

_____

Concluding Sentence _____

_____

_____

_____

Alike and Different

Write the title of your paragraph on the line below. Then use your "alike and different" paragraph plan from page 38 to write your paragraph.

_____

_____

_____

_____

_____

_____

_____

_____

_____

_____

_____

_____

_____

Assessment

Write a paragraph about any subject you choose. After you choose your topic, make a list of ideas. Next, develop a topic sentence for your paragraph, put your list of body sentences in order, and write a concluding sentence. Write your paragraph plan below.

After you have written your paragraph, be sure that you have your details in the best order.

Where you think it is necessary, add specific details. Be sure to remove any unrelated details.

Then, check for ways to combine sentences and vary sentence structure. Also, check for ways to improve word choice. Be sure that all your words are specific and exact.

Finally, proofread your paragraph. Check for errors in grammar, punctuation, capitalization, and spelling.

You may write your paragraph on the back of this page or on a separate sheet of paper.

_____

_____

_____

_____

_____

_____

_____

_____

_____

Paragraph Checklist

Use this checklist as part of the process whenever you write a paragraph. You should also use it as a guide when you write your paragraphs.

- ☐ Prewriting, planning, organizing
- ☐ One main idea or topic
- ☐ List of supporting details in order
- ☐ Topic sentence developed
- ☐ Supporting details sentences developed
- ☐ Concluding sentence developed
- ☐ Unnecessary details removed
- ☐ Supporting details added
- ☐ Varied sentence structures
- ☐ Grammar checked
- ☐ Punctuation checked
- ☐ Spelling checked

Paragraph Organizer

Write your topic idea in the center of the oval. Then write the details you want to include on the lines or spokes. To organize a paragraph first, write a topic sentence. Then write the details in an order that makes sense. Add a concluding sentence to finish your paragraph.

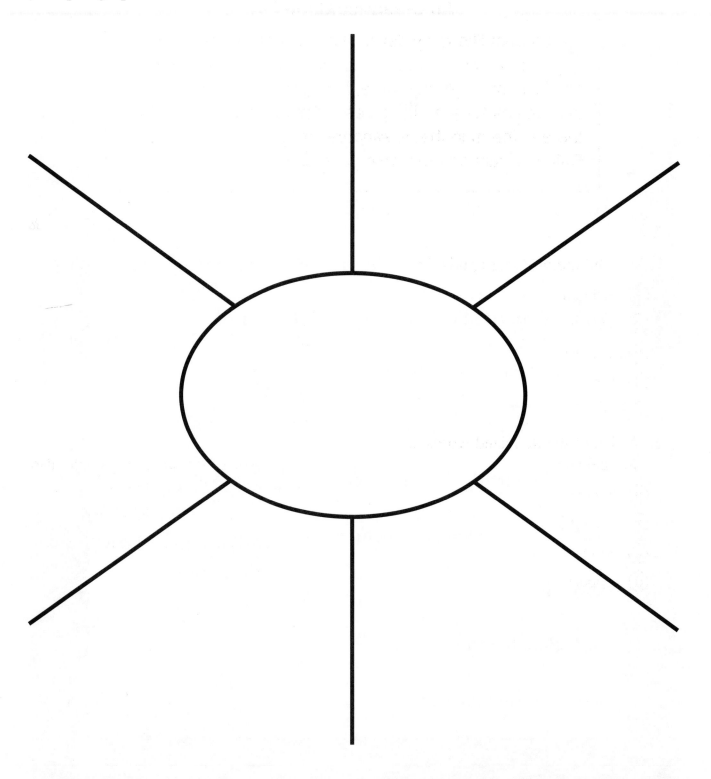

Unit Assessment

Read the paragraph and answer the questions that follow it. Fill in the circles beside the correct answers.

> ### An Otherwise Good Day
>
> I do not like rainy days. Rain may make the *flowers* grow, but it only makes me soggy and *miserable*. First of all, if I want to go anywhere, I will get wet. Then the gray *clouwds* make everything seem dim and dreary. Finally, there is the mud that is *slippery* and gets everything dirty. Rain can ruin an otherwise good day.

1. Which kind of paragraph is this?

   ⓐ explanation

   ⓑ description

   ⓒ persuasion

   ⓓ story

2. Which of the italicized words is misspelled?

   ⓐ flowers

   ⓑ miserable

   ⓒ clouwds

   ⓓ slippery

3. How many sentences make up the body of this paragraph?

   ⓐ 1

   ⓑ 2

   ⓒ 3

   ⓓ 4

4. Which one of the following could also be the title of the paragraph?

   ⓐ Sunny Days Warm My Heart

   ⓑ Every Day Is a Good Day

   ⓒ Rainy-Day Blues

   ⓓ The Blue Guitar

Unit Assessment (cont.)

The sentences in the following paragraph are numbered and are not in the proper order. Answer the questions about the sentences in the paragraph by filling in the circles beside the correct answers.

I Want to Fly

(1) It is really fun when the <u>plane</u> takes off. (2) Airports are very interesting <u>places</u>. (3) I can get to <u>sue's</u> house really fast in an airplane. (4) I love to fly! (5) I want to be an <u>airline</u> pilot when I grow up.

---

1. Which sentence is the topic sentence?

   ⓐ 1
   ⓑ 2
   ⓒ 3
   ⓓ 4

2. Which sentence is the concluding sentence?

   ⓐ 1
   ⓑ 2
   ⓒ 3
   ⓓ 5

3. Which one of these sentences could fit into the body of the paragraph?

   ⓐ Everybody enjoys good music.
   ⓑ My grandmother has two dogs.
   ⓒ My friend wants to be a firefighter.
   ⓓ The feeling I get when I fly is different from any other.

4. Which underlined word should begin with a capital letter?

   ⓐ plane
   ⓑ places
   ⓒ sue's
   ⓓ airline

Unit Assessment (cont.)

This incomplete paragraph has words that can be replaced with more specific and exact words. Choose words to replace the italicized words. Fill in the circles beside the correct answers.

> ### Big Fat Cat
>
> The other day I saw a *big* cat. That fat cat was *walking* down the street all by herself. She had an enormous tail that she *moved* back and forth. Along with an immense tail, she also had *big* paws.

1. big
   - (a) tiny
   - (b) huge
   - (c) muscular
   - (d) wooden

2. walking
   - (a) skipping
   - (b) scampering
   - (c) singing
   - (d) pointing

3. moved
   - (a) tingled
   - (b) carried
   - (c) waved
   - (d) raced

4. big
   - (a) silly
   - (b) gigantic
   - (c) clumsy
   - (d) pointed

Unit Assessment (cont.)

Each sentence in the following paragraph is numbered. Read the paragraph and then answer the questions about it by filling in the circles next to the correct answers.

My Magic Bottle

(1) If a genie popped out of my magic bottle, I would ask him for three wishes. **(2)** First, I would ask him to make me a genius? **(3)** Next, my request would be to be really strong. **(4)** Then, I would ask him to change my personality so that everyone who meets me would want to be my friend. **(5)** Finally, I would ask him to make me 10 years older than I am now.

---

1. Which title also fits this paragraph?

   (a) If My Genie Appears
   (b) Everybody Needs a Genie
   (c) Jeanne Grants My Wishes
   (d) Gene Won a Prize

2. Which of these pairs of sentences could trade places?

   (a) 1 and 5
   (b) 4 and 5
   (c) 3 and 4
   (d) 2 and 3

3. Which of these words acts as a guide to let you know that you are in the middle of a paragraph?

   (a) first
   (b) next
   (c) finally
   (d) last

4. Which sentence has the incorrect punctuation mark at the end?

   (a) 1
   (b) 2
   (c) 3
   (d) 4

Answer Key

page 5
1. I saw Danny in Dayton, Ohio. (declarative)
2. Did you see Fran in Dallas, Texas? (interrogative)
3. Do not go to Europe by yourself. (imperative)
4. What a great time they had! (exclamatory)
5. Jan and Vicky run in races.
6. She runs faster than he does.
7. Gwen and George carefully stepped into the gleaming red circus wagon.

page 6
Mornings
1. wake up
2. wash face
3. hang up towel
4. get dressed
5. comb hair
6. eat breakfast
7. catch bus
(Accept logical variations.)
Baking a Cake
1. find recipe
2. preheat oven
3. gather ingredients
4. measure ingredients
5. mix batter
6. pour batter in pan
7. put cake in oven

page 7
(Accept logical ideas/details.)
1. Ice Cream
2. Favorite Rides
3. Summer
4. School

page 8
All ideas/details listed must be about the topics.

page 9
1. **Television Shows**
   Disney movies
   Saturday morning cartoons

2. **Best Subjects**
   math
   language arts
   social studies
3. **My Pet**
   keeps me company
   goes everywhere with me
   easy to please

page 10
1. **Olympics Events**
   marathon
   gymnastics
   swimming
2. **My Brother**
   two years older
   teases me
   helps me with math
3. **Our House**
   on a quiet street
   friendly neighborhood
   large family room

page 11
1. **Rainy-Day Activities**
   write letters
   read books
   bake cookies
2. **My Allowance**
   spend some, save some
   have to earn it
   paid weekly
3. **Winter Activities**
   snowball fights
   make snowmen
   ride sleds

page 12
Sample topic sentences
1. Marshmallows are very delicious.
2. My pet is the sleepiest cat around.
3. Swimming is not for me.

page 13
Sample body sentences
1. Never make your bed.
2. It seems to me my dog is easier to work with than my cat.

page 14
Sample concluding sentences
1. All these things make school a good place to be.
2. We should be glad there are firefighters to put out dangerous fires and rescue people.

page 15
1. S
2. S
3. T
4. S
5. S
6. C

page 16
Sample topic sentence
I can usually think of interesting things to do on rainy days.
1. S
2. S
3. S
4. S
5. S
6. C

The very first thing I do is write a letter to my Grandmother Lucille. She lives far away in London, England. My next activity of the day is to make two dozen delicious cookies. My favorite books are adventure stories. After I have made my favorite chocolate cookies, I find a good book to read. These pleasures keep me busy for an entire rainy day.

page 17
Sample topic sentence
Leslie and I have a good time in the snow.
supporting details
First, Leslie and I have snowball fights.
Next, we do one of our favorite projects.
We build a snowman.
Then, after we build a snowman, we ride down the

hill on our sleds.
sample concluding sentence
These are the things that help Leslie and me enjoy the snow.

page 18
Rainy Days
2, 3, 1, 4, 5
Homework Afternoons
5, 1, 3, 2, 4
Our Excellent House
1, 3, 2, 4, 5

page 19
Sample sentences
1. Everyone but Shawn went to the movie.
2. Do you want to roller skate or play soccer?
3. I know how to read and write.
4. Would you like milk or water?
(Note: These answers avoid compound sentences and the use of the comma with the conjunction. Ex.: Everyone went to the movie, but Shawn did not.)

page 20
Sample varied sentences
My Early Morning
When I wake up at six o'clock, I hop out of bed and get ready for school. I go downstairs. After I eat breakfast, I grab my schoolbooks and go outside to wait for the bus. Charlotte is the friend I sit with on the bus. Next, I arrive at school and walk with my friends Charlotte and Molly to the classroom. My early morning ends there.

page 21
Rainy-Day Activities
1. c
2. c
3. a

Answer Key (cont.)

page 22
Wintertime Fun
- a. 3
- b. 5
- c. 8

page 23
sample
Huckleberry Finn Park
Huckleberry Finn Park is the park where I like to go. It has 11 different swings and three different slides. There is also other playground equipment. The park has many trees that are easy and fun to climb and a place where I can have a picnic. My favorite park to go to when I want to play and to picnic is Huckleberry Finn Park.

page 24
Camping Is Fun
Camping is fun for many reasons. It is fun to sleep outside or in a tent. Food tastes better when it has been cooked over an open fire. One of my favorite camping foods is the s'mores we make with graham crackers, marshmallows, and pieces of chocolate. Also, it is exciting when I see a deer or another wild animal from my campsite. Besides watching the animals, I like to hike in the woods and fish in the river. At the end of the camping day, I like to sleep in a cozy sleeping bag. All these things make camping fun.

page 25
1. Grant and Stuart put their toys away every night.
2. Nancy ran across the street in front of the car.
3. Casey does not like to play with dolls.
4. Yesterday Michael was too sick to go to New York.
5. Today Ezra also did not feel well.
6. Will Jenny be ill tomorrow?
7. Let's hope that both of them are okay.

page 26
Meadow Monkeys
In the meadow you will find many animals, including the harvest mouse. This tiny animal can climb from plant to plant and looks just like a monkey. Harvest mice climb these plants looking for food. They eat as much as they can in the summer to get ready for winter.

page 27
Snake in the Grass
A snake is one of the scariest animals. The grass snake likes to rest in the sun. Grass snakes eat frogs and newts. They live in marshy meadows. Sometimes the grass snake will pretend to be dead. The more you learn about snakes, the less scary they are.

page 28
I Need My Sleep
Today I woke up early, got out of bed, and brushed my teeth. After that, I put my homework in my backpack. I ate breakfast, but then I noticed that it was very quiet. First, I went to my mom's room, but she was still sleeping. Next, I went to my brother's room, but he was still sleeping, too. When I went to the porch, I saw that even the dog was still sleeping. Suddenly, I remembered it was Saturday, so I went back to bed!

page 29
Sample edit
Kyle and Kate went to the zoo where they saw many different animals. First, they saw a cage filled with rattlesnakes. Next, they saw a pen with a mother giraffe and a baby giraffe in it. A young elephant eating peanuts was in the last pen. Kyle and Kate enjoyed seeing all the animals at the city zoo.

page 30
Sample edit
The *Gigantic* Spider
I spied the *gigantic* spider on my *bedroom* desk. Slowly and *carefully*, I sneaked around my *cluttered* desk, gazing at the *scary* spider. "What is the spider doing on my *messy* desk?" I thought to myself. Where had the *terrible* spider come from? Which one of my *mean* enemies planted the spider on my sloppy desk? As I tiptoed toward my *horrible* desk, the ugly spider began to move. I screamed *loudly* and dashed from my *untidy* room.

page 31
Sample edit
My Baby Brother
My baby brother is a pest. He is always sneaking into my room and making a mess there. Yesterday he sneaked into my room while I was at school. First, he ripped all of the pages out of one of my favorite books. Then he messed around in my closet and pulled all my clean clothes off the hangers. To top it off, he pulled out into the middle of the floor all my treasures I had hidden under my bed. Never should my baby brother creep into my room. Forever is too short a time to keep him locked out of my room.

page 43
1. a
2. c
3. d
4. c

page 44
1. d
2. d
3. d
4. c

page 45
1. b
2. b
3. c
4. b

page 46
1. a
2. c
3. b
4. b